KU-176-338

# One-Minute Prayers

*Text by Hope Lyda*

HARVEST HOUSE PUBLISHERS

EUGENE, OREGON

Page 12: Psalm 138:8 brackets are in original

Page 110: The second Scripture quotation is Isaiah 9:6

*Cover by Garborg Design Works, Minneapolis, Minnesota*

*Cover photo copyright © Getty Images*

**ONE-MINUTE PRAYERS™**
Copyright © 2004 by Harvest House Publishers
Published by Harvest House Publishers
Eugene, Oregon 97402
www.harvesthousepublishers.com

ISBN-13: 978-0-7369-1283-9 (pbk.)
ISBN-10: 0-7369-1283-5 (pbk.)
Product # 6912835

**Printed in the United States of America**

06  07  08  09  10  11  12 / BP-MS / 15  14  13  12  11  10

# Contents

# You Began a Good Work

*In all my prayers for all of you, I always pray with
joy because of your partnership in the gospel from
the first day until now, being confident of this, that
he who began a good work in you will carry it on to
completion until the day of Christ Jesus.*

—PHILIPPIANS 1:4-6

When the bedside alarm sounds, concerns left over
from yesterday clutter my mind. A list of things to do
surfaces on my mental planner. Then come the choices.
What to wear? Which road will have less traffic this morning? Tea, juice, coffee…decaf? latté? extra shot?

When did starting a day become so complicated?

Wait. My heart knows the answer to this one. I recall
a time when mornings began with one decision: to
spend time with You. Your Word smoothed the way. The
priorities for the day fell into place. The simple choices
did not distract me—I could step into work of significance. Let me start this day over, Lord. I feel Your presence pointing me in the right direction. I am ready.
Confident. For You began a good work in me, and I will
walk with You until it is completed.

*Purpose*

# Exchanging My Plans for God's

*Many are the plans in a man's heart, but it is the*
*LORD's purpose that prevails.*

**—PROVERBS 19:21**

જી

Lord, how many times have You heard me say, "So much to do, so little time"? When I catch myself repeating this mantra, it is followed by a shrug of resignation. Lord, is it the plight of humans to be so busy with plans for improvement, gain, success? My culture tells me it is so. God, shake the foundations of self-absorbed plans. Reveal to me the purpose You have for me, my time, my money, my work, my family, my today.

Take my tightly held heart. Reshape it. Let it expand to fit that place You have made for me in this world. Help me to not settle for a life of busyness that does not make room for what I should be doing. You have something far greater for me to grow into: Your purpose for my life.

# My Purpose in Your Church

*If you have any encouragement from being united with Christ, if any comfort from his love, if any fellowship with the Spirit, if any tenderness and compassion, then make my joy complete by being like-minded, having the same love, being one in spirit and purpose.*

—PHILIPPIANS 2:1-2

Lord, help me to be like-minded with my community of fellowship. Guide me to compassion when in the presence of others' pain. Let me tend to people with the love You give. Empower me with a spirit of willingness to work with Your children.

I see a display of Your character wherever people are gathered, Lord. Our differences balance into wholeness through Your grace. It can be so difficult to look past the human idiosyncrasies. They distract us. They give us excuses to place people in categories or push them away. Let me see a person as a whole being. A physical, intellectual, and spiritual child of God. I pray that my actions will always help and not hinder the body of Christ's progression toward Your purpose.

10

# How God Works

*We know that in all things God works for the good of those who love him, who have been called according to his purpose.*

—ROMANS 8:28

Lately, not many things seem to be working together for good, Lord. I am not complaining, just stating it like it is. But of course, I don't see as far down the road as You do…and perhaps a few of these situations just didn't work out in *my* favor. As I revisit the circumstances, maybe these moments were not about my personal success, but someone else's. Did I handle it well, Lord? I pray for a sense of Your grand vision. Help me take every disappointing event, answer, and outcome and look at it from Your perspective. I may not see evidence of Your plan, so let me rest in my knowledge of Your love. Grant my heart peace when I am uncertain of the road I travel, Lord. I will keep moving, one foot in front of the other, because I have been called to good things.

# What's Next?

*The Lord will fulfill [his purpose] for me; your love,*
*O Lord, endures forever—do not abandon the works*
*of your hands.*

—PSALM 138:8

Don't stop now, Lord. I am finally catching Your vision for my life. It has taken me a while, and I've had to walk through a lot of mistakes, but I am here and ready to receive Your purpose. What would You have me do next? Your patience over the years has shown me that You will not abandon the work You have begun. Lead me to the next step.

When I listen to others or even to my own negative thoughts, I am tempted to quit trying. Your love inspires me to keep going. And each time I move forward, my step is more steady. I am certain You will follow through. And I will follow Your example. So, what's next?

*Gifts*

# According to God's Grace

*We have different gifts, according to the grace given us. If a man's gift is prophesying, let him use it in proportion to his faith. If it is serving, let him serve; if it is teaching, let him teach; if it is encouraging, let him encourage; if it is contributing to the needs of others, let him give generously; if it is leadership, let him govern diligently; if it is showing mercy, let him do it cheerfully.*

—ROMANS 12:6-8

Lord, which gifts have You given me? I do not want to waste a drop of my life by being blind to my potential in You. I seek a deeper understanding of Your Word. I want to comprehend how You manifest Yourself through spiritual gifts in Your children. I long to explore the lives of men and women in Scripture who followed You and who actively lived out their gifts.

<u>According to the grace given me, I can live a fruitful life.</u> I can share the amazing bounty of Your goodness with others. Help me to pay close attention to the work You are doing in my own heart. I want to see, understand, and cultivate the gifts that come from You.

# Different Gifts of the Same Spirit

*There are different kinds of gifts, but the same Spirit.*
*There are different kinds of service, but the same Lord.*
*There are different kinds of working, but the same*
*God works all of them in all men.*

—CORINTHIANS 12:4-6

❊ Lord, I stand in awe of Your love that is so great…so great that You have made each one of Your children unique, special, and miraculous. Our differences are not discerned just in physical characteristics or the language we speak, they are found in a kaleidoscope of gifts—all from the same Spirit.

Often my weakness is another's point of strength—my certainty, another's roadblock of doubt. You have created us to work together. Help me to acknowledge the gifts of others. I want to encourage the people I interact with to do and be their best…Your best. Guide my words, Lord, so that I express kindness and inspiration to my family, colleagues, and friends.

# All I Have

*As he looked up, Jesus saw the rich putting their gifts
into the temple treasury. He also saw a poor widow
put in two very small copper coins. "I tell you the
truth," he said, "this poor widow has put in more than
all the others. All these people gave their gifts out of
their wealth; but she out of her poverty put in all she
had to live on."*

—LUKE 21:1-4

Forgive me for how tightly I hold on to the blessings my life. I am too cautious in my giving. I even
question how the one I give to will use my offering, as
if that has anything to do with what giving is about.
Along the way I have forgotten that giving is an act of
sacrifice. It is an offering without strings, an expression
of Your grace.

I don't want to hold back, Lord. I want to freely
stretch out my hand to provide help, a blessing, a
commitment to another. Prevent my heart from moni-
toring, counting, adjusting what I give. May I never keep
track of such things. With Your gift of salvation as my
only measure, I pray to give all I have in every moment.

# These Are My Gifts

*On coming to the house, they saw the child with his mother Mary, and they bowed down and worshiped him. Then they opened their treasures and presented him with gifts of gold and of incense and of myrrh.*

—MATTHEW 2:11

I open the treasure of my heart and look for gifts to give You, my King. My offerings reflect the ways I worship You each day. *Love* for my family. *Kindness* to others. *Help* in the face of need. *Faith* in the future. *Trust* through doubt. Lord, please accept these as responses of my deep affection for You.

I bow down to You, Lord. Your grace transforms my simple presents into precious metals and expensive oils and perfume. Help me to watch for opportunities to serve You by giving the gift of myself to others. And let me recognize when I am receiving treasured pieces of another's heart.

*Direction*

# Following Directions

*Walk in all the way that the LORD your God has commanded you, so that you may live and prosper and prolong your days in the land that you will possess.*

—DEUTERONOMY 5:33

Lord, from Your vantage point, the charting of my daily course must look like a very unorganized spider's web. Here. There. Back again. How many days do I spend running in circles to keep up with the life I've created? Lead me to the life *You* planned for me. Unravel those strands of confusion and weave together a course that is of Your design.

This new vision for my life involves asking You for directions. Remind me of the beautiful pattern my steps can create when I seek Your help—when I feel lost *and* when I feel in control. Lord, give me the insight to follow Your commands. Guide me toward my true life.

# The Guiding Force of Nature

*He loads the clouds with moisture; he scatters his lightning through them. At his direction they swirl around over the face of the whole earth to do whatever he commands them.*

—JOB 37:11-12

Lord, Your hand choreographs the dance of nature. You speak forth the rhythm of the ocean waves. Your word commands the clouds to rain on the thirsty land. The precise action and inaction of every element is under Your instruction. Why do I challenge the force of Your will in my life? I need only to witness the power of a stormy day or watch the sun dissolve into the horizon to know that You rule over all living things.

The beauty of creation can be mirrored in my own life. I must first give myself over to the dance that You choreograph. May I leap with full joy. Let my sweeping bow mimic Your grace. And as I stretch heavenward with open arms, may I be ready to receive the loving commands You rain down on me.

# Moving into God's Love

*May the Lord direct your hearts into God's love and Christ's perseverance.*

**—2 THESSALONIANS 3:5**

Lord, I confess I have been playing tug-of-war with You. As You start to pull my heartstrings in one direction, I stubbornly resist. Goals and aims other than Your best dazzle me with cheap imitations of love. I avert my gaze for just a moment and lose sight of Your plan. Instill in me a steadfast heart. Let me be single-minded in my faith and trust.

Allow me to persevere in the direction You want me to go. Let me not be tempted by false gods or deceptive voices, which lead me astray. I should never play games with my heart. After all, it belongs to You. Take it now, Lord. I don't want to halt the beat of Your love in my life.

# A Parent's Instruction

*My son, keep your father's commands and do not forsake your mother's teaching...When you walk, they will guide you.*

**—PROVERBS 6:20,22**

"Don't touch the stove." "Look both ways." "Don't hit your sister." "Say you're sorry." Lord, the earliest instructions from my parents became lessons for my spiritual growth. The concept of cause and effect seeped past my resistance. Eventually I saw how parental guidance was about protection and concern.

Your commands reflect this truth from my childhood. I know that You guard my steps because You love me. I look to You before I proceed with a plan. I await Your approving nod before I make commitments and promises. Your Word lights my way even when I have run so far ahead that Your voice seems faint. Lord, may I always hear and heed Your directions. Guide me toward a righteous life.

*Confidence*

# Certain of Your Protection

*Have no fear of sudden disaster or of the ruin that overtakes the wicked, for the LORD will be your confidence and will keep your foot from being snared.*

—PROVERBS 3:25-26

The world feels out of control, God. I watch the news and turn away. But later, the fear of ruin, or violence, or disaster seeps into my soul. I am awakened by the pounding of my heart. While my daily routine finishes, I am anxious and unsettled. Lord, help me to place my confidence in You. I long for the peace You offer.

When I look to You, my spirit is soothed. Replace the list of dangers that runs through my mind with words of assurance. Let me witness Your hand on my life and in all circumstances. Turn my scattered worries into passages of prayer. When I see the world's pain, may I not use Your protection as a reason for isolation. Let me tap into Your love for empathy, compassion, and prayers of "Thy will be done."

# Always My Hope

*You have been my hope, O Sovereign LORD, my confidence since my youth.*

—PSALM 71:5

When I first came to know You personally, Lord, I stood so tall. I had unshakable faith in Your mightiness. When I am around a new believer, I feel that excitement once again. Restore this confidence, Lord. I will turn to the wisdom of Your Word and infuse my life with the security of Your promises.

Thank You, Lord, for the power You extend to me. The small windows of opportunity I once perceived are now wide-open doors. Everything is better when I stand in Your confidence. Fortify my life with the strength of Your plan. As I rise up to claim my hope in You, let me stand tall…just as I did in the youth of my faith.

# He Hears Me

*This is the confidence we have in approaching God:
that if we ask anything according to his will, he hears
us.*

—1 JOHN 5:14

Lord, thank You for hearing me. Your ears are open to the musings of my heart, the longings of my soul, and the questions of my mind. There is nobody else in my life who promises to hear every part of me. Even in my most insecure moments, I utter words I know will reach Your heart. I dwell on worries my friends would not take seriously. I have fears that, brought up in daily conversation, would sound unreasonable. Yet, You listen.

It is a gift to be vulnerable with the Creator. You are my Master, yet I can come to You with the simplest needs or concerns. As Your child, I seek Your will and Your response. As my Father, You listen.

# Without Shame

*Now, dear children, continue in him, so that when he appears we may be confident and unashamed before him at his coming.*

—1 JOHN 2:28

Purify me, Lord. My sinful ways build up pride and lead me to worship idols of money, status, and success. I have tried to hide my blemishes, my stains, but that is a false life. I want the life You have laid out for me. It is spotless and clean. It is a life to honor.

As You work out Your purpose in me, may I never be boastful or arrogant. This detracts from You, the Source of my confidence—and others will not understand that You are the Master of all that is good in my life. Let my mouth be quick to praise Your grace, which has removed my shame, healed my wounds, and made me whole.

# The Past

# Communication
# Then and Now

*In the past God spoke to our forefathers through the
prophets at many times and in various ways, but in
these last days he has spoken to us by his Son, whom
he appointed heir of all things, and through whom
he made the universe.*

—HEBREWS 1:1-2

God, You had a communication plan in place at the
inception of the universe. You knew Your children
would need to hear Your voice. There are times I wish
that Your prophets were still so easily recognized. Yet,
would I even listen in this day and age? Likely, I'd bustle
right past a proclaimed prophet in my hurry to catch
the subway.

Lord, You know the shape of the past and the shape
of things to come. You saw that the world would need
a relationship with Your Son. A personal Savior to wake
us up from our blurry, busy lives. I see You, God. I hear
You. And I thank You for keeping the line of communication open through the power of Your Son.

# Hope for the Future

*Everything that was written in the past was written to teach us, so that through endurance and the encouragement of the Scriptures we might have hope.*

—ROMANS 15:4

Lord, the wisdom of the lessons found in Your Word speaks to my life today. I thank You for the fresh hope that breathes through words scribed so many years ago. I am amazed how Scripture moves me. Some people try to cast it away as irrelevant, but they have not immersed themselves in Your truths.

You care so much for me, for all of Your children, that You created an unending source of encouragement and instruction. Help me to stay grounded in the teachings of the Bible, Lord. Show me the opportunities I have to live out the lessons of Scripture. I want to be an active student of Your love and Your ways.

# The Rains Are Over

*See! The winter is past; the rains are over and gone.*
*Flowers appear on the earth; the season of singing*
*has come.*

**—SONG OF SOLOMON 2:11-12**

Days of hardship and pain have rained down in my past, Lord. There were storms that destroyed the foundations I had built. Floods swept away the hope I had placed in material things and in the strength I thought I saw in others. All that remained was the washed-out land of disappointment. But that was in the past. A time when I could not see a future.

Now the flowers sprout and shout from the earth. They sing a song of Your faithfulness. This is a new season for me, Lord. Past sorrows fade away and future hopes and dreams grow strong. You offer me this renewal every day, Lord. I am grateful for the rains, for they have prepared my soul to receive the blessings.

# Moving On

*Forget the former things; do not dwell on the past.*
*See, I am doing a new thing! Now it springs up; do*
*you not perceive it?*

—ISAIAH 43:18-19

Free me from the past, Lord. I spend too much time there. Good times that have come and gone replay in my mind so often that I miss the wonder of today's joy. Cause me to return to the present, Lord. Draw my attention back to the life in front of me. My past has nothing to offer You or myself. But today...now...has so much to offer.

Give me a view of new wonders You are doing. I imagine they are brilliant happenings. Do not let my mind slip to the past, except to count the times You have blessed me. Then I must move on. My past serves my future...it is a foundation for all days that follow. Now, I must invest my time, my dreams, my prayers on the future You have carved out for me.

*Preparation*

# Nourishment from Your Table

*You prepare a table before me in the presence of my enemies.*

—PSALM 23:5

When I face the opposition of the enemy, Lord, I can run to the table You are preparing for me. I am seated beside You—and I drink of Your wisdom, I eat of Your truth, and I am satisfied. I am saved here at Your table. My enemies and worries fade in the presence of my Host.

At each sitting I am nourished by Your banquet. When I leave the table to face my day, Your goodness follows me. I am filled with Your satisfying love. When I fear my enemies, I think of the security of Your eternal home. I shake my head in amazement that You promise to protect me, prepare the way for me, and reserve a place for me at the table of Your grace. You welcome me into Your presence, and I am blessed.

# Prepared for Action

*Prepare your minds for action; be self-controlled; set your hope fully on the grace to be given you when Jesus Christ is revealed.*

**—1 PETER 1:13**

I try to exercise so that I am physically prepared for the demands of my daily life. But, Lord, I need help to prepare my mind and heart for the requirements of the spiritual life. I read Your Word and carry those lessons with me, but I admit I am still very weak. I face trials and still rely on my own strength rather than on the mightiness of Your power. I lose faith in Your ability to overcome my difficulties.

Lord, help me to truly be prepared. I need to go beyond head knowledge and claim a heart courage. Will I let myself fall back into Your arms when I feel weak, certain that You will catch me? Today, I am prepared to try.

# A Room of My Own

*In my Father's house are many rooms; if it were not so, I would have told you. I am going there to prepare a place for you. And if I go and prepare a place for you, I will come back and take you to be with me that you also may be where I am.*

—JOHN 14:2-3

I remember the first time I had my own room. Even at a young age, I felt a sense of being cared for and provided for. Lord, I spent so much time preparing every detail in order to make it unquestionably mine. I think of this experience when I read Your promise to prepare a room for me. A place for me in heaven's glory.

When You take me home and show me this room, I am certain it will reflect how well You know my heart. The walls will be the shade of happiness. The fabrics will be woven with threads of loving memories. It will shimmer with Your splendor. I will run into it gladly, eager to be in Your presence forever. And I will know that the Master of the house prepared this room because I am unquestionably His.

# A Ready Heart

*Create in me a pure heart, O God, and renew a stead-fast spirit within me.*

—PSALM 51:10

Just as You prepare a place for me, Lord, may I prepare a place for You. Create in me a clean heart that is pleasing to You. Make it a place that welcomes Your presence. God, I want a heart that clings tightly to Your promises. Let it beat strongly with Your purpose.

I want my soul to be a fortress that holds and protects Your Word within. Design a temple that is worthy to be called Your home. As I move through my days, I will think of the One who resides in me. Fill my heart with all that is pure and right so it will not be sacrificed to false gods but will be preserved and prepared for You alone.

*Trust*

# Relying on You

*Pay attention and listen to the sayings of the wise; apply your heart to what I teach, for it is pleasing when you keep them in your heart and have all of them ready on your lips. So that your trust may be in the LORD, I teach you today, even you.*

—**PROVERBS 22:17-19**

Trusting in You changes everything, Lord. I will not dwell on past failings, and I won't wager on things to come. Because right now is my most important time frame. Allow me to worship You better. Help me to seek Your ways more earnestly. Let my thoughts and my actions be pure in Your sight, Lord. I will heed the lessons of the wise.

I see the day ahead and imagine ways to improve. I will look for people who need encouragement, including myself, and will recite words of Your faithfulness. I will watch for the opportunities and unique moments You offer that teach me more about You. Yes, I told myself yesterday I was not worthy of Your love...but the assurance of the sunrise this morning spoke of Your grace. I trust You, Lord.

# A Song to Sing

*I trust in your unfailing love; my heart rejoices in your salvation. I will sing to the L*ORD*, for he has been good to me.*

**—PSALM 13:5-6**

God, You have been so good to me. I trust You and what You are doing in my life. Some days I clearly see Your love for me. I received a kind word at a time of sorrow. I was offered help when I was afraid to ask. And just when I thought I could not continue, I had a vision of what Your hand was doing in that very circumstance.

I could not navigate my days without trusting Your love and intent for good. I pray that my actions translate into lyrics for the world to hear. I want everyone to know the song of Your love and mercy. I lift up my voice to proclaim Your goodness. "I know a love that never fails me!" I cry out into a world of people who know only of broken love and misplaced trust. Thank You, Lord. For giving me a song to sing.

# You Are Mine

*I trust in you, O LORD; I say, "You are my God."*
—PSALM 31:14

∽

Lord, I want my lips to praise You in all situations. No matter the circumstances I am in, I want my first thoughts to be of praise, because I trust You with my life. May everything I do be a witness to this trust. When people around me attempt to fix my problems with temporal solutions, I will stand firm in my belief.

How often do I say, "You are my God"? Do my actions speak this? Do my relationships reflect this truth? I want every part of my life to resound with this statement. When Your peace replaces my worry, I want others to hear the reason. Let it be clear to people I meet that my trust is placed only in You. Help me to say it loudly, even in the silent moments that follow difficult times.

# Entrusting a Soul

*To you, O LORD, I lift up my soul; in you I trust, O
my God. Do not let me be put to shame, nor let my
enemies triumph over me.*

—PSALM 25:1-2

In a moment of possible failure, Lord, am I trusting You to save me—or to save face for me? Help me
lift up my soul without requirements and requests. I trust
You to work out this situation for good, not evil. My
humanity begs me to avoid humiliation at all costs, but
I know I will be saved for different reasons: My weakness becomes evidence of Your strength. My destruc-
tion turns into a testimony of Your instruction and mercy.

Do not let me shame You, Lord. Let this moment
shine light upon Your goodness. May it cast shadows on
my need for recognition or reputation. Please accept this
offering of my soul. There are no strings attached—only
complete trust and gratitude come with this sacrifice.

*Perspective*

# A Goal in View

*A discerning man keeps wisdom in view, but a fool's
eyes wander to the ends of the earth.*

—**PROVERBS 17:24**

Okay, Lord, sometimes I become anxious about the
plans I have under way. I start seeing the success that
could follow. Or the different paths my life might take.
What if this? What if that? I could end up here. Or there.
Distracted by the possibilities, I step a bit to the side,
turn without noticing, lose my balance. I become blind
to Your priorities.

Lord, help me to keep Your wisdom in view. When
my eyes start to scan the horizon of grand illusions, I
lose perspective of what is right and reasonable. Guide
me, Lord. Place Your hand on my shoulders and direct
me. Give me discernment to keep my eyes trained on
Your will.

# Through a Worldly Lens

*From now on we regard no one from a worldly point of view. Though we once regarded Christ in this way, we do so no longer. Therefore, if anyone is in Christ, he is a new creation; the old has gone, the new has come!*

—2 CORINTHIANS 5:16-17

The eyes of a homeless man caught my attention today, Lord. They narrowed in the heat of the day and looked past me. I wondered when begging became necessary for him to survive. Did he have a family waiting for him at a shelter? Was his mother a worried, heartsick woman miles away? When was the last time he was comforted? I saw his thin, ragged figure through Your eyes, just for a moment, Lord, and I did not see a beggar—I saw a child of Your own.

A worldview through rose-colored glasses offers a selective look at pain, poverty, and need. Lord, I pray to adopt Your viewpoint. Let my heart have a vision of its own when I stand face-to-face with a child in need. The responsibility of a new vision scares me. But I stand before You, ragged and poor in spirit, and ask You to help me.

# Looking Straight Ahead

*Forgetting what is behind and straining toward what
is ahead, I press on toward the goal to win the prize
for which God has called me heavenward in Christ
Jesus. All of us who are mature should take such a
view of things. And if on some point you think differ-
ently, that too God will make clear to you.*

—PHILIPPIANS 3:13-15

Lord, You know that thing I was worrying about last
year? It has just surfaced again. It was a speck in the
corner of my mind, and now it has taken over my field
of vision. I fixate on it between phone calls and errands.
Please help me strain toward what is ahead rather than
dwell on what has ended. I want to press on toward
the goal of a godly life.

Make it clear to me, Lord, when I am wasting
precious time on matters of the past. You call me to go
forward, to head toward eternity with assurance and
purpose. Please, Lord, I want to exchange my life of limi-
tation and blindness for Your ways of freedom and
vision.

# Examine Me

*A man's ways are in full view of the LORD, and he examines all his paths.*

—**PROVERBS 5:21**

It is painful for me to think about past mistakes. Because of the many sins that occupied my days and my ways, I missed opportunities. But that is not the difficult part...I know I have saddened Your heart, Lord. You watched me make those choices. You saw me choose pride over submission. I failed You and myself more times than I even know. But You know.

I have asked forgiveness of these past sins, and You forgave. Now, Lord, teach me Your way. Examine my new paths and find them holy and pleasing to You. When I get off course, pull me back to Your will. When I lose sight of my goal, show me Your perspective and lead me to examine my heart at every turn.

# Dependence

# Freedom Through Dependence

*If anyone acknowledges that Jesus is the Son of God,*
*God lives in him and he in God. And so we know*
*and rely on the love God has for us.*

—1 JOHN 4:15-16

Only You, Lord, offer me deep love. I dive in and feel Your presence all around me. We are a part of one another. Creator and creation. I am so blessed to have met and accepted the gift of Christ. This relationship is sufficient for all my needs. This love has covered my iniquities. Dependence has given me freedom and a path to eternity.

When I meet someone in pain, I want them to know Your love. How do they make it, if not with You? Even a life filled with blessings encounters stumbling blocks. Lord, next time I am hurt, broken, and weak, immerse me in the depths of Your mercy. As I surface and struggle for air, I depend on Your breath of life to fill my being.

# I Trusted You Before
# I Knew You

*From birth I have relied on you; you brought me forth
from my mother's womb. I will ever praise you.*

—PSALM 71:6

Lord, You were there when I was formed in my
mother's womb. You knew my heart, my character, my
purpose as I was brought into the world. I was so
defenseless then, so vulnerable. I know Your hand was
upon my life for every minute. Even before I had a
personal relationship with You, I relied on You
completely.

Now I am so established in the world and can appear
strong and in control. But I confess I am as vulnerable
as the day I was born. I praise You for the countless times
You have protected me, saved me without my knowledge. O Lord, Your loving hand was and will be with
me every step of the way. I am so glad to be Your child.

# He Is My Mighty Rock

*My salvation and my honor depend on God; he is*
*my mighty rock, my refuge.*

—PSALM 62:7

Lord, You tower over my life. Your presence intimidates my enemies. You are my refuge during times of trouble. When I experience days of doubt, I climb onto Your rock of refuge. I stand against the wind and view my fretting from new heights. I see You crush my worries in the shadow of Your strength. I need not be afraid.

You are my safe place, Lord. I rise to sit on Your shoulders when I feel small. I lean against the weight of Your power and restore my strength. You are my security at all times. God, my life requires Your authority. I want You to reign over my days. Help me build a spirit of perseverance and a character of honor on the foundation of Your goodness.

# See My Pain

*Turn to me and be gracious to me, for I am lonely and afflicted. The troubles of my heart have multiplied; free me from my anguish. Look upon my affliction and my distress and take away all my sins.*

—PSALM 25:16-18

Lord, see the depth of my pain. I am facing difficulties, and I feel alone as I seek solutions for my problems. Just as I put out one fire, I smell the smoke of another about to burst forth in flames. There has been so much. I don't know where to begin...except at the foot of Your cross. Free me, Lord. Take my anguish and my affliction and have mercy on my soul.

These problems that are surfacing—many are caused by bad decisions made in haste and without Your guidance. Forgive me, God. This isn't the first time I have been overwhelmed by trouble. Lord, give me strength. Turn to me and see the repentance in my eyes and heart.

*Giving*

# The Reluctant Servant

*The precepts of the LORD are right, giving joy to the heart.*

—PSALM 19:8

༃

Lord, when I was a child, I hated being told what to do. If asked to perform a chore, I resisted, found distractions, or muddled my way through it. Guidelines felt like punishment. I knew I was capable of doing the things that were asked of me—I just wanted to do them in my own way. I gave of myself in my own time frame.

How often do I resist Your precepts, Lord? I see the right way to give or serve, yet I fight it. I don't want to change my plans or be inconvenienced. I have had a reluctant heart, Lord, and I am sorry. Help me to follow Your commands with a giving spirit. I have asked many times before, but I still long to have a joyful heart that follows Your way.

# Giving Light

*God said, "Let there be lights in the expanse of the sky to separate the day from the night, and let them serve as signs to mark seasons and days and years, and let them be lights in the expanse of the sky to give light on the earth."*

—GENESIS 1:14-15

Some people light up a room. I know Christians who reflect Your radiance everywhere they go, Lord. I want this kind of luster in my life. Show me how to give off a light that illuminates a moment. My faith needs to be polished to a sheen so that it sparkles and reflects Your face.

Guide me into action, Lord. Don't let me fall into a dark pit of apathy and make a home there. The further I distance myself from Your light, the less likely I am to be reignited in my passion for Your will. Most of all, I want my hope in You to give light to others. Help me shine, Lord.

# Private Donations

*When you give to the needy, do not let your left hand know what your right hand is doing, so that your giving may be in secret. Then your Father, who sees what is done in secret, will reward you.*

—MATTHEW 6:3-4

ക

It is hard to resist taking credit, Lord. Truth is, I am taking credit away from You every time I seek acknowledgment for giving my time, energy, or money. I feel so utterly human when I want affirmation. Isn't it enough to know that You see me and are pleased? Lord, help me to desire heaven's praise above all else. Guard me from a pretentious existence that feeds off recognition or success.

Any time I reach out to give to another, I am giving from Your source of plenty, not from any abundance I have created on my own. The credit is Yours to have. Humble my spirit so that the blessing of giving resides in my heart—in secret, under Your proud gaze. Pleasing You, Lord, is the only reward I desire.

# Praise You

*Speak to one another with psalms, hymns and spir-
itual songs. Sing and make music in your heart to
the Lord, always giving thanks to God the Father for
everything, in the name of our Lord Jesus Christ.*

—EPHESIANS 5:19-20

Praise You. My spirits are lifted just saying that to
You. So why am I quick to squelch the music of my soul?
Some time ago, I told myself that songs and praises were
shallow and emotional. Forgive me—Lord, I have forgotten that rejoicing is not frivolity—it is an offering to You.

I have held my tongue for too long. I will raise my
hands to the sky. I will lift my voice to the heavens, and
I will give You praise, Lord, for You are worthy. Hear
my hymn of thanksgiving, Lord, for all You have done
and are doing in my life. I will not silence my spirit in
Your presence again.

*Letting Go*

# I'm Pouting

*These people have stubborn and rebellious hearts;*
*they have turned aside and gone away.*

—JEREMIAH 5:23

I won't. I won't, Lord. Not just yet. I know I should let go of my recent behavior, but I just don't feel ready. You could make me, but You choose not to. Now, my choice is to pout for a while. My fingers are turning white as I grip this thing I will not release to You. I have a headache and really would rather rest. When did I become so difficult?

Sure, I'm shaking a little bit. My arms are growing weary. This is, after all, a heavy burden. I think I will set it down for a minute...just long enough to get some lunch. Without that huge anchor around my heart, I could take care of a few things after lunch. I sure feel better, Lord.

I'm picking it up again—this time to hand it over to You, Lord. I get it...when I let go of such things, I am free. I am choosing to be free, Lord. Thank You for waiting.

# Come Near to Me, Lord

*Submit yourselves, then, to God. Resist the devil, and
he will flee from you. Come near to God and he will
come near to you.*

—JAMES 4:7-8

Submission is one of those concepts that bothers me,
Lord. If You must know, it causes me to feel quite threatened. Help me to see the security that follows submission. I want to be under Your authority, Your control,
Your cover of love. Forgive me for being tied to my identity as a self-made person. I have strived so long for
control of my life that it feels unnatural to give it over
to You.

Release me from my fear of submission, Lord. It has
created a wall between us. Please come near to me.
Empower me with the strength to resist the temptation
to remain in control. I look forward to claiming the identity of a God-made person.

*Prayer*

# Prayers for Healing

*This is what the LORD, the God of your father David,
says: I have heard your prayer and seen your tears;
I will heal you.*

—2 KINGS 20:5

I weep in private, away from the well-meaning
inquiries of friends. And You, Lord, see my tears.
Awkward, shattered expressions of pain and confusion
stumble from my lips, yet You heal the words. My prayer
is whole when it falls upon Your heart. Your answer is
complete: You love me. You see me. You will heal my
brokenness.

It must be difficult to explain the ways of life and
loss to Your children. When I ask "Why, Lord?" You do
not turn away from me and my neediness. You hold me
close and show Your heart. It is broken too—You have
taken my pain. I watch Your tears fall and understand
they have healed me.

# Merciful Lord

*The LORD has heard my cry for mercy; the LORD accepts my prayer.*

—PSALM 6:9

I walked around numb and in denial for months, Lord. My façade was perfect. I didn't miss a beat at work. I stood in the grocery store express line and not one soul looked at me with pity. I encouraged a hurting friend with words that I myself could not yet accept about You: "You are a merciful Lord."

Then my heart spoke up. It sent out an SOS cry for mercy and compassion on my behalf. Lord, thank You for accepting this prayer. I could not gather the courage or energy to bring You my burdens. I was sick and tired of myself, but You raised me out of the trap of self-pity. I am a new creation. I accept the truth about You: You are merciful, Lord.

# Prayer Song

*By day the LORD directs his love, at night his song is with me—a prayer to the God of my life.*

**—PSALM 42:8**

I sing to You, Lord. My joy, heartache, and thanksgiving create a symphony of emotion. In the solitude of nightfall, I cannot help but sing. I release the worries of my day to Your care. I trust You with my today and my tomorrow. My panic turns to peace as the first notes of praise drift heavenward.

Your concern touches me. Your voice blends with mine for a few sweet moments. You wrote this song to comfort me every night. You share it with me so I can come to You when the confines of words and dialogue stifle meaning. By day, Lord, guide me with Your love. By night, free me with Your melody. In every moment You are the God of my life.

# True Devotion

*Devote yourselves to prayer, being watchful and thankful.*

—COLOSSIANS 4:2

God, can You work with me on my commitment issues? Build in me a desire to pray. I want to be a disciplined follower. Steady my spirit to stillness. Quiet and solitude prepare me for Your presence. Direct my eyes to be watching for Your answers, watching as my prayers are heard and responded to. I want to see and recognize Your work in my life.

Cause my faith to grow, Lord. Each day that I come to meet with You, may I know You better. Replace my ignorance with Your knowledge. Help me be strong in my commitment to You. Show me how to pray, Lord.

*Faithfulness*

# I Am Your Child

*The living, the living—they praise you, as I am doing today; fathers tell their children about your faithfulness.*

**—ISAIAH 38:19**

Lord, I live today as Your child. I plan to focus on this identity. Undoubtedly I will be asking for guidance, messing things up, getting Your pristine plans dirty, and constantly asking, "Why? Why?" But You are used to the floundering of Your children. You are a patient parent. The lessons You have taught me in Your Word and through Your active love are helping me grow. I can see the person You want me to become.

Like a child, I will run in lots of different directions before asking the way. And by then, I will probably need to be carried. It is very exhausting being a child. But now, as You lift me up and comfort me with Your promise of love and grace, I settle down. To be wrapped in Your faithfulness is all I needed...I just didn't know how to get there. When I am done resting, will You tell me a story? I love the one about the day I became Your child.

# Finding My Way Home

*Love and faithfulness meet together; righteousness and peace kiss each other. Faithfulness springs forth from the earth, and righteousness looks down from heaven.*

—PSALM 85:10-11

At the intersection of Your love and faithfulness, Lord, I have found my life. For years I have taken many detours. My soul longed for intrigue, so it turned down curious, narrow avenues; I found only pain and suffering. My spirit craved success and celebrity, so I ventured along the flashy main streets, only to find failure and isolation.

Then I stopped following my "wants" and listened to my heart. My pace quickened as I caught a glimpse of the crossroads ahead. You waited patiently for me on the corner. I didn't ask what it was You were promising or how long it would last. I could see home in Your eyes, and it went on forever.

# Flawless and Faithful

*O Lord, you are my God; I will exalt you and praise*
*your name, for in perfect faithfulness you have done*
*marvelous things, things planned long ago.*

**—ISAIAH 25:1**

I did not give You much to work with early on in my life, Lord. What a sight I was back then. Rumpled, tough, stubborn, and ignorant. "Just try to do something with this!" I challenged You on a particularly bad day. I was acting out the courage found in movie heroes, but my heart was really pleading with You, *"Please—do something with my life."*

You answered this cry for help because You knew I would someday step into Your faithfulness and be transformed into a shining, perfect child of God. You turned my spirit of spite into a heart of praise. Praise You, Lord. Long ago You planned such marvelous things for my life. I cannot wait to see where Your faithfulness will lead.

# **Your Creation Endures**

*Your faithfulness continues through all generations;*
*you established the earth, and it endures.*

**—PSALM 119:90**

Beneath my feet is proof of Your commitment, Lord. You established the earth and set it in motion to serve Your children and Your greater purpose. Your creation speaks of Your enduring faithfulness. God, the lineage of just one family has countless testimonies of Your limitless love.

I pray that I will carry on stories of Your holiness to others in my family. Let my praises spread to those in my spiritual family. May I then speak of Your goodness to those who do not yet know You. May I always be a faithful child who models the faithfulness of my Father.

# Blessings

# Receiving God's Blessing

*May God give you of heaven's dew and of earth's richness—an abundance of grain and new wine.*

—GENESIS 27:28

I have had my share of goodness, Lord. I need only to look at my immediate surroundings and the people in my life to see how richly I have been blessed. Why do I pay such close attention to the imperfections of my life? *My job could be more important. My family could be a bit more agreeable. My body could be in better shape, like the woman on that television show. My car could be newer and have all of those extras I saw on the commercials that interrupted that television show.* You see how my mind starts to destroy all the blessings?

Lord, open my eyes to the good in all situations. Let the times of poverty I experience cause me to embrace the richness of Your bounty. Help me to be aware of the manna that falls from heaven and lands in my life.

# Satisfied by Grace

*From the fullness of his grace we have all received
one blessing after another.*

—JOHN 1:16

I look at the life You have given me, Lord, and I see
great blessings. You have provided for my needs. Your
grace has allowed me to reach goals. There is so much
more I want to do, but I have learned to wait on Your
timing. There is an order to godly things. When I let
Your priorities guide my journey, blessings build upon
blessings.

Hold me back when I try to force advancement,
Lord. I don't want anything in my life, even if it resembles success, if it is not from You. I pray for discernment
to know the difference between aspirations fabricated
by my heart and those born of Your will. Free me from
thoughts of envy, judgment, and greed. I want to be satisfied by Your grace alone.

# Inherit a Blessing

*Do not repay evil with evil or insult with insult, but*
*with blessing, because to this you were called so that*
*you may inherit a blessing.*

—1 PETER 3:9

Lord, I am more likely to hold a grudge than release
a blessing when someone has hurt me. My reaction to
conflict reveals how desperately I need Your forgiveness
to flow through me. Heal me from the anger that rises
so quickly. I want to reflect Your image to others, even
those who are working against me.

Let me ponder Your holiness before facing a poten-
tially difficult encounter or situation. I want to arm myself
with Your Word, Your strength, and Your compassion
so I can honor Your name with my actions. I will inherit
a blessing by spreading the legacy of Your love.

# Find Me Righteous

*Surely, O LORD, you bless the righteous; you surround*
*them with your favor as with a shield.*

—PSALM 5:12

Search my heart, O Lord. May You find it righteous
and pure. I long for joy in my life. This season of hardship has tempted me to question how Your blessings
are given. What have I done to deserve this pain? But
my heart knows I am forgiven—Your mercy covers my
sins. How can I use this time to draw closer to You rather
than challenge Your mercy?

What do You want me to learn from my life today?
Alleviate my confusion. Pierce my heart with Your love.
Encourage me with the security of believing friends.
Saturate my days with evidence of blessings yet to come.
Surround me with Your favor. Protect my fragile heart.

*Opportunity*

# Embracing the Unknown

*Show me your ways, O LORD, teach me your paths;*
*guide me in your truth and teach me, for you are God*
*my Savior, and my hope is in you all day long.*

—PSALM 25:4-5

Father in heaven, You see all that takes place in my life. Knowing this gives me peace as I face transition. I exchange my uncertainty for Your promise of security. Open my eyes to the wonders of every turn, tangent, and seeming detour I encounter. I don't want to miss a miracle by starting a new journey diminished by regret, pride, or misplaced longing. I want to long for You. For the path You carve out for me.

Remove the blinders from my physical and spiritual eyes, Lord. I want to see the beauty of the landscape You have built around me. And I want to savor the opportunity that rests on the horizon. As I face a new direction, this time my heart flutters with excitement and not with worry. I am eager to see what You have in store for me. I accept Your provision, Lord.

# Doing Good

*As we have opportunity, let us do good to all people, especially to those who belong to the family of believers.*

—GALATIANS 6:10

Where can I do the most good, Lord? Direct me. Guide me to the people You want me to serve. I used to give only to random causes and organizations. My offering at church became my "I gave at the office" excuse when other needs arose. Then, Lord, You allowed me to personally experience small kindnesses. I came to understand how the little matters mean the most. Create a clean motive in my heart, God. May I do good purely to honor You, and not my own reputation.

Help me reach out and establish real relationships. Even if my encounter with a person is for one day, one hour, one smile, this is my opportunity to serve You. I will wait, watch, and act on these opportunities.

# Choosing Peace

*If it is possible, as far as it depends on you, live at peace with everyone.*

—ROMANS 12:18

Lord, I long for Your peace in my soul. I wish to draw it in and release it to others. Where I have a chance to act out Your peace, please let me be strong and brave. Conflict is easier sometimes. It allows me to build barriers between me and another, or between me and the right way. But there is little comfort when I stand alone, indignant on one side of the wall.

May I meditate on Your Word so that it rises to my mind in place of angry and defensive language. Peace flows from You and into my life. I know its power to change behavior and remove blindness. Grant me the opportunity to share this gift.

# Opportunity of a Lifetime

*He replied, "You are talking like a foolish woman.*
*Shall we accept good from God, and not trouble?"*

—JOB 2:10

When my timeline, career, family life, and spiritual walk are going as planned, I accept Your ways, Lord. I rest in how rewarding my faith can be. But when I face hardship, I assume You have left me or have caused me pain. I know this is not truth. You do not give us more than we are able to bear. God, help me sense Your active presence. Teach me Your mercy so that I never question it again. Give my heart a measure of promise to keep me going.

Plant in me a trust that will take firm root. Help me recall the previous times when difficulties turned into lessons, strength, and even blessing. May I see every obstacle as an opportunity to accept *all* that You have for me.

*Grace*

# Living Grace

*Each one should use whatever gift he has received
to serve others, faithfully administering God's grace
in its various forms.*

—1 PETER 4:10

༺

"God works in mysterious ways." People say that.
I say that. But as I examine life, Lord, I see You also work
in practical, concrete, anything-but-mystical ways. A
friend comforted me during a recent stretch of bad days.
A stranger helped me change a flat tire on the freeway
during rush hour. The clerk at the video store found
and returned my lost wallet. Everyday happenings, upon
observation, are really vignettes of Your grace.

People sharing their gifts of empathy, kindness, and
honesty express Your love. Lord, when I feel that same
tug on my heart, let me be faithful in following through
with Your direction. I see how honoring the gifts You
have graciously given is really about making connec-
tions with Your other children. Your mercy is found in
the most mundane situations, and when we least expect
it. Help me to watch for Your living grace.

# Rich with Redemption

*In him we have redemption through his blood, the
forgiveness of sins, in accordance with the riches of
God's grace that he lavished on us with all wisdom
and understanding.*

**—EPHESIANS 1:7-8**

Keep me from being spiritually poor, Lord. In the
material realm, I want for nothing. I have food to eat
and a roof over my head. I have the means to care for
my family. I even have tasted the luxury of abundance.
But it takes wisdom to amass spiritual riches. Lead me
to understand the treasures of salvation.

Your love inspires and satisfies me, Lord. I have been
redeemed through the sacrifice of Christ. Your grace
leads to spiritual riches. It multiplies to cover every one
of my iniquities. My soul was purchased for a price, and
it has made me a wealthy child of God.

# I Work So Hard

*It is by grace you have been saved, through faith—
and this not from yourselves, it is the gift of God—
not by works, so that no one can boast. For we are
God's workmanship, created in Christ Jesus to do good
works, which God prepared in advance for us to do.*

—EPHESIANS 2:8-10

I work so industriously, God. There is sweat on my
brow as I survey the fruits of my labor. Signs of my hard
work are everywhere. I dedicate the work of my hands
to You. And yet, I resist the one thing You call me to
do right now—fall to my knees and accept Your grace.
Why is that so difficult for me, Lord?

Soften my heart to receive Your saving grace.
Eliminate in me the need to earn Your love. You freely
give Your grace so I can focus on doing the good works
You have prepared for me. Grant me a deeper understanding of Your provision. And receive my humble
spirit as I rest in Your mercy.

# Approaching the Throne

*Let us...approach the throne of grace with confidence,*
*so that we may receive mercy and find grace to help*
*us in our time of need.*

—HEBREWS 4:16

I am stepping out in faith, Lord. I hold my hands out to You with expectation. Pour Your grace over me. Let it cover me, fill me, and then overflow from me. I need You today, Lord, more than ever before. I walked around for months in false confidence based on my ability. It fell apart. As soon as one stone was cast at my façade, I came crumbling down in fragments of dust and pride.

Breathe Your mercy into my soul. Let my body depend on it more than oxygen. Rebuild my life according to Your plan. Only then can I return to You with confidence to ask for help, ask for Your grace, ask to be whole.

*Love*

# Love One Another

*Let no debt remain outstanding, except the contin-
uing debt to love one another, for he who loves his
fellowman has fulfilled the law.*

—ROMANS 13:8

God, I pray for renewal in my relationships with
family and friends. My heartstrings are tied to so many
people that I sometimes lose sight of the uniqueness and
privilege of each individual relationship. Guide my
thoughts and my prayers so that I would be discerning the needs of those You have brought into my life.
May I see how each friend and family member is a part
of the body of Christ.

When I need encouragement and laughter, draw me
to those who offer such nourishment. I thank You for
the people in my life who bring comfort, who pray for
me, and who are examples of Your love. Some connec-
tions are fragile and tenuous, others are deeply rooted
and mighty; I pray for wisdom to know how to nurture
each one.

# All My Heart

*Hear, O Israel: The LORD our God, the LORD is one.*
*Love the LORD your God with all your heart and with*
*all your soul and with all your strength.*

—DEUTERONOMY 6:4-5

Lord, give me the capacity to love fully, completely.
I hold back. I stay aloof on matters of the heart when
I should be diving in headfirst. When I look at the cross,
I know You have shown me the deepest depths of mercy.
Sacrifice. Forgiveness. Salvation. Help me embrace this
model of perfect love and live it each day.

Maybe because I know I can never repay You for
Your mercy, I resist trying to return Your love. Please
accept my offering of love. It will not be all You deserve,
but I will try. Your Word and Your living example inspire
me to greater passion. I want to be consumed by my
love for You, Lord, until You possess all of my heart and
soul.

# Better than Life

*Because your love is better than life, my lips will glorify you.*

—PSALM 63:3

My favorite things in life are examples of Your perfect beauty. A sky so blue it reflects peace. Friendships so strong they mirror Your faithfulness. Happiness so deep it encompasses Your joy. I cannot separate You from these miracles of life, because You are at the core of them. And as much as I cherish these gifts, I know Your love for me and for Your creation is even more vibrant.

Lord, I praise Your presence in every remarkable thing. Your radiance illuminates the miraculous in each moment. May I sing Your praises all the day long. May my lips glorify You because there is nothing better than Your love.

# You Heard Me

*I love the LORD, for he heard my voice; he heard my cry for mercy. Because he turned his ear to me, I will call on him as long as I live.*

**—PSALM 116:1-2**

I don't need to take anyone's word for it, Lord—I know You answer prayer. I love to hear of others who have called out to You, and how You soothed their pain…but I don't need those examples for assurance. I know of Your goodness and mercy. I have been the one to call out in desperation. At times when I felt the most undeserving of Your attention, You turned Your ear to me and were faithful.

You reach out to me in my darkest hour and You hold me, comfort me, and see my sorrow. Your compassion is a balm for my soul. My tears fall freely at the thought of Your unconditional love. I don't need to be convinced of Your mercy, because when I cried out to You, my Lord, You heard me.

*Seeking*

# Heart and Soul

*Now devote your heart and soul to seeking the LORD your God.*

—1 CHRONICLES 22:19

Lord, do I pursue You as I should? I have had hobbies take over my life. Do I give You the same attention? I spend countless hours perusing bookstores and immersing myself in the riches of the written word. When was the last time I gave my spiritual quest the same amount of energy? It's been a while.

I realize I have become lax in my pursuit of You, Lord. You and my faith should occupy my mind more than a part-time interest. Infuse my soul with a desire to pursue You wholly. Completely. I want to know everything about You. I hunger for Your Word. I devote my heart and soul to seeking You and Your will for my life.

# Name Above All Names

*Those who know your name will trust in you, for you,*
*LORD, have never forsaken those who seek you.*

—PSALM 9:10

I know Your name so well, Lord. I whisper it in times of sorrow. I hold it close when entering a place of fear. I shout its praise during times of celebration. You have carved it on my heart so that I will never forget the Creator of my soul. I do not go anywhere without being covered by Your name, for it is powerful.

When I experience doubt, Lord, remind me that "he will be called Wonderful Counselor, Mighty God, Everlasting Father, Prince of Peace." You are all these things to me, Lord. Let me never forget to call on You, the One who does not forsake me but leads me to higher places.

# Thoughts of God

*In his pride the wicked does not seek him; in all his thoughts there is no room for God.*

—PSALM 10:4

Lord, reveal to me where I am prideful. What causes me to stumble while trying to do Your will? Obstacles that grow in size and threaten to become permanent in my life hinder my view of Your face. Even though it will be painful, please remove these barriers to a holy life.

Heal me from blindness caused by too much self-focus. When my eyes turn only toward my own life, I lose sight of the future You have for me. My worries weigh me down and immobilize me when I should be seeking Your freedom. Lord, please take away my selfish thoughts. They crowd out Your voice, the voice that gives me purpose.

# Justice for All

*Many seek an audience with a ruler, but it is from the LORD that man gets justice.*

**—PROVERBS 29:26**

I want to be heard, Lord. I always want to tell my side of a situation so an authority can vindicate me. But it is You, Lord, who should receive my call for justice. You are the judge of my soul and my life—why should I seek out any other rulers? In the same way, help me to resist determining the fate of another. It is not my right to stand in Your place.

Lord, guide me in Your ways when there is conflict. Fill me with wisdom, honesty, and courage, and let me rely on their strength if I am accused. Keep me blameless so no harm is brought to Your name. Guard my heart from resentment if I am not treated fairly. May I live out forgiveness and faith, anticipating the justice of love I will receive when in Your presence.

*Faith*

# Restored by Faith

*He touched their eyes and said, "According to your faith will it be done to you"; and their sight was restored.*

—MATTHEW 9:29-30

Heal me, Lord, from the inside out. My spirit is sick from worry and stress. Create a healthy soul inside this temple. I have neglected to nourish my spirit—show me the way back. Wounds ignored for too long need Your healing touch. Remove scars that remind me of old but not forgotten hurts. I trust You to mend my brokenness.

Let me have the same belief when I need physical healing. I know You hear and answer these prayers. Help me to understand that I do *not* understand the vast number of ways in which You heal. My human eyes can be blind to Your acts of mercy. Restore my sight, Lord. Let me feel Your touch and hear You say, "According to your faith will it be done to you."

# Facing the Storm

*Without warning, a furious storm came up on the lake, so that the waves swept over the boat. But Jesus was sleeping. The disciples went and woke him, saying, "Lord, save us! We're going to drown!" He replied, "You of little faith, why are you so afraid?" Then he got up and rebuked the winds and the waves, and it was completely calm.*

—MATTHEW 8:24-26

Craziness consumes me, Lord. Frantic days filled with discussions, arguments, and anxieties I cannot even recall a day later. Beneath the confidence I show the world, God, You know an ocean of fear rocks and swells. I feel it when I spend a few minutes in silence. That is why I avoid quiet time with You. I'm afraid to face the storm.

God, I am just like the disciples who followed You and listened to Your many explanations of what it means to believe. I have heard Your parables and witnessed Your faithfulness, yet I cry, "Save me," with little faith. Pull my gaze to Your eyes. Do not let me look at the waves about to crash into my ordered world. When the winds die down and I face You on the calm waters, I want to be found standing as a faithful servant.

116

# Nothing Is Impossible

*"I tell you the truth, if you have faith as small as a mustard seed, you can say to this mountain, 'Move from here to there' and it will move. Nothing will be impossible for you."*

—MATTHEW 17:20

All-powerful Lord, Your might is a part of my life. The incredibleness of this truth is my reason for often neglecting Your resource. How can it be possible that You allow Your children such strength? What an awesome God You are. History shows us that kings of men often strip their followers of hope. But You clothe those in Your kingdom with possibility.

Show me what faith, even the smallest faith, can accomplish, Lord. Next time I face a mountain on my spiritual journey, I will not ask if You will help me to the top. Instead, I will draw forth a faith that requires the obstacle be moved altogether.

# Promises to Others

*Have we not all one Father? Did not one God create
us? Why do we profane the covenant of our fathers
by breaking faith with one another?*

—MALACHI 2:10

I want to be a keeper of promises. Lord, lead me to
make only commitments I am strong enough to fulfill.
Good intentions cause me to step up to meet many
needs. But I have discovered something…I am not a
good judge of time and responsibility. Forgive me for
letting down even one other person. Free in Your mercy,
I do not have to live a life buried in guilt—but I do desire
to be honorable before others and You.

Guard me from becoming overconfident and inde-
pendent. That is when I take on too many demands.
Protect me from breaking bread with a friend one day,
then breaking faith with them on another. Bless me with
a heart whose generosity is followed by perseverance
and commitment.

# The Future

# Your Perfect Will

*Do not conform any longer to the pattern of this world, but be transformed by the renewing of your mind. Then you will be able to test and approve what God's will is—his good, pleasing and perfect will.*

—ROMANS 12:2

So many choices and decisions seem to fill my world, Lord. I pray to rest in Your will and Your way so that I do not lose sight of my future as a child of God. My work can consume me, and my worries about material things can undermine the blessings. Change my heart, Lord. Let the matters of eternal importance become my priority list.

Oh, how I crave a life of significance. But even as I pray, a flood of insecurities can fill me, and I have no room left for the purpose You wish to pour into my cup. Let me not be anxious to fill my life with clutter and trivial distractions, Lord. Let my life, my heart, my soul be vessels that await the flow of Your Spirit.

# Release Me from Worry

*Who of you by worrying can add a single hour to his life? Since you cannot do this very little thing, why do you worry about the rest?*

—LUKE 12:25-26

Lord, You are my source of strength in all things. How do I forget that Your mighty hand is placed upon my life? Today, I give over to You the many things that occupy my mind and my heart. Help me to release my worries to You as they take hold of me. These anxieties keep me from embracing the life You have planned for me. Your mercy surrounds me with comfort. Your love is my source of strength, and it is my future.

Meet me today, Lord. Here in this moment. In the midst of the troubles that weigh me down. Sometimes it is difficult for me to ask for help. To admit to weakness. But my soul is weary, and I want to give my burdens over to You. You are a mighty, faithful God. Thank You, Lord, for hearing my prayers today and every day. My spirit is buoyed as my prayers are spoken. I love You, Lord.

# Hope and a Future

*"I know the plans I have for you,"* declares the LORD,
*"plans to prosper you and not to harm you, plans to
give you hope and a future."*

—JEREMIAH 29:11

My to-do lists and the task reminders that pop up
on my computer screen reflect a bit of my nature. Lord,
I like to know what will occur and how it will take place.
No surprises for me, please. I equate the unknown with
potential problems. Cure me, Lord, of such a pessimistic
view of my future. I have hope…I just want control too.
It is so very shortsighted of me to have such little trust
in You, the Creator of the world and of my life.

Reach out and still my active, worried mind so it
receives and accepts Your Word. You have plans to prosper me and not to harm me. Replace my anticipation
of complications with assurance of security. May I start
and end my to-do lists with prayers of thanksgiving.

# Self-Talk

*I am convinced that neither death nor life, neither*
*angels nor demons, neither the present nor the future,*
*nor any powers, neither height nor depth, nor any-*
*thing else in all creation, will be able to separate us*
*from the love of God that is in Christ Jesus our Lord.*

—ROMANS 8:38-39

If I could have a conference call with my past self, present self, and future self, I believe I would discover one truth: Your love has always been with me. The voices of my self over the course of my life would share stories about testing Your commitment. I tried to measure Your love by running far from heaven's reach. I stretched Your love by pushing the boundaries. I shoved away Your love when my doubt tried to poke holes in Your truth.

And Your love remained.

I have many questions about my future, but after listening to the course of my life, one thing is certain— my heart will never be separated from the love of its Creator.

*Miracles*

# Something Remarkable

*Everyone was amazed and gave praise to God. They were filled with awe and said, "We have seen remarkable things today."*

—LUKE 5:26

Lord, I confess I have been thinking about how unremarkable my life is. I wake up, I go to work, I try to be a good friend and a loving member of my family, but nothing extraordinary takes place. It is just me, moving through the daily necessities.

Lord, forgive me…I have forgotten how remarkable it is to breathe in and out, to be alive. Somehow I have ignored the privilege of true joy. And how many times have I been amazed by Your compassionate covering of my hurts? Each day that I move deeper into the future You have planned for me is a miracle of renewal. Praise You, Lord, for You are doing remarkable things in my life today. Sometimes I just need to be reminded.

# Tell the World

*"Everybody living in Jerusalem knows they have done
an outstanding miracle, and we cannot deny it. But
to stop this thing from spreading any further among
the people, we must warn these men to speak no
longer to anyone in this name."*

—ACTS 4:16-17

So many around the world and throughout history
have tried to silence Your name, Lord. But Your name
and the gospel of salvation continue to reach across
continents and into the hearts of people. I think of Your
disciples, who were asked not to discuss the miracles
performed through Your power. They were warned and
threatened, yet they said they could not help speaking
about all they had seen and heard. They faced risk and
still remained true to You.

I thank You for freedom to share my faith. I can
talk about the miraculous love I have experienced.
Encourage me to use this blessing. Give me the courage
to be a disciple who refuses to silence the sound of
a miracle.

# Because I Believe

*Does God give you his Spirit and work miracles among you because you observe the law, or because you believe what you heard?*

—GALATIANS 3:5

Lord, I believe You and I believe in You. This is my foundation as I read about Your miracles in Scripture. But the power behind such wonders is more than people of that day or our day can fathom. God, I acknowledge that I too want to place the works of Your hand up against the laws of man and nature and scrutinize them. Just a little.

Even today, I read of miraculous moments that are evidence of Your work—and I must first fight the urge to see if there is another explanation. Help me to believe what I hear and read. Give me discernment in such matters so I can fully embrace the signs of Your Spirit at work today.

# Climate Control

*He did not do many miracles there because of their
lack of faith.*

—MATTHEW 13:58

Lord, heal me from my disbelief. A climate of faith
welcomes Your wonders. Has my lack of faith kept You
from performing a miracle in my life? It is hard for me
not to be cynical sometimes. I start by being frustrated
about the condition of the world, my city, my family,
or my self—then, I let these feelings bleed over into my
faith. Do not let me taint my spirit any further, Lord.

Restore to me a faithful heart, Lord. Lead me to people
who are encouragers and who counter the apathy that
builds up in my daily life. I want to be overflowing with
faith. I want to be ready to receive a miracle.

*Abundance*

# Telling of Your Goodness

*They will tell of the power of your awesome works, and I will proclaim your great deeds. They will celebrate your abundant goodness and joyfully sing of your righteousness.*

—PSALM 145:6-7

Lord, Your awesome works are everywhere. Goodness flows through many channels but comes from You alone. Strengthen my spirit so I will be bold when speaking of Your greatness. I can be shy about sharing You. Or sometimes it seems self-righteous of me to mention my faith. Lord, guide my heart to speak truth at all times. Let my words never be forced, but free-flowing from You, the Source of all goodness.

When I share about You with others, help them discover and celebrate Your abundant love and mercy. Give me a voice to sing of Your righteousness. Direct my path toward those who need to hear the good news. And when I forget it in my own life, remind me of this prayer and the praises I feel in my heart today.

# With or Without

*I know what it is to be in need, and I know what it
is to have plenty. I have learned the secret of being
content in any and every situation, whether well fed
or hungry, whether living in plenty or in want. I can
do everything through him who gives me strength.*

—PHILIPPIANS 4:12-13

Lord, Your hand has guided me through times of
want and times of plenty. I thank You for being my
Source of strength and guidance. When I hungered for
more and thirsted for opportunity, I followed Your way
to brighter days. You guided me through years of abundance so that I could be a devoted steward of my blessings. My status in the world's eyes might change, but
my relationship with You remains the same.

Teach me about contentment, Lord. When I have
material wealth, may I still long for spiritual direction
and nourishment. As I experience difficulties, lead my
thoughts and prayers to You for direction and hope. I
can do all things and survive all circumstances through
Your strength.

# Dream-Come-True

*He who works his land will have abundant food, but he who chases fantasies lacks judgment.*

**—PROVERBS 12:11**

I have a hard time staying focused. Any bit of dazzle catches my eye. When someone passes by who is living the life I covet, I turn my head and watch them walk away. Fix my mind on the work in front of me, Lord. Return my attention and intentions to the many important and wonderful pieces of my life.

When my head is in the clouds, dreaming of what I want or think I need, pull me back into the abundant day You have given me. I have family, friends, health, and You. The tasks I face today will reap rewards that are real—not just material pleasures, but emotional treasures like satisfaction, fulfillment, contribution, meaning, and purpose. I'll keep dreaming, Lord, but I will ground my days in my dream-come-true: Your unconditional love.

# What's Mine Is Yours

*O LORD our God, as for all this abundance that we have provided for building you a temple for your Holy Name, it comes from your hand, and all of it belongs to you.*

—1 CHRONICLES 29:16

Everything I create, Lord, is Your creation. My best ideas are manna from heaven. The life I am building is a temple that belongs to You. May I give You all and understand that You are the Source of every good thing I have. When I sit back and look fondly at my family, I know they are a gift from You.

Free me from the burden of owning things, Lord. I will keep up my responsibilities and tend to whatever is in my care, but release me from the desire to claim things as my own: *I want. I need. I must have.* This train of thought is getting old. I want to rest in knowing You own all things. Blessings come from Your hand, and that is where I in turn will place them.

*Provision*

# Daily Bread

*Give us today our daily bread.*
—MATTHEW 6:11

Lord, I give You my entire day. I humbly lift up the sacrifice of my daily living to be used to Your glory. This empty vessel will be filled with strength, courage, hope, and blessing...Your provision flows like living water, and it is plentiful. May others see that You are the One who gives me life and who provides for my daily needs. You, who are the bread of life, do not let any one of Your children go hungry.

Where there was nothing in my life, there is now a bounty of goodness. Dry land has turned to thriving pastures. And when I grow hard toward such blessing and cry out for more in the presence of so much, remind me that the daily bread You give *is* enough. Let my heart open up to Your gracious gifts. And may each day I give to You be worthy in Your sight.

# Refreshment

*You gave abundant showers, O God; you refreshed*
*your weary inheritance. Your people settled in it, and*
*from your bounty, O God, you provided for the poor.*

—PSALM 68:9-10

I grow weary on my journey sometimes. You have carried me often, Lord. I have felt used and useless when going through a rough spot—a dry existence that lacks nourishment and substance. Anything I try to grow just withers and blows away toward the horizon…far away from me.

I look back on these times of my journey. You have sent showers of refreshment in many ways—opportunities appeared when I doubted their existence, kindness humbled me and my bad attitude, and abundant love flooded through me. Your provision has brought me back to life. My path continues, and I am no longer afraid of the droughts I may face along the way.

# Learning to Share

*Command those who are rich in this present world*
*not to be arrogant nor to put their hope in wealth,*
*which is so uncertain, but to put their hope in God,*
*who richly provides us with everything for our enjoy-*
*ment. Command them to do good, to be rich in good*
*deeds, and to be generous and willing to share.*

—1 TIMOTHY 6:17-18

Who can follow the stock market? I get really
confused. I feel left behind in the race for wealth. Keeping
up with the Joneses isn't the standard anymore—everyone wants to keep up with movie stars and computer
moguls. Lord, help me out of this cycle of depravity.
Make me rich in my love for others. Direct my longings
back to You and Your wealth of spiritual abundance.

Lord, I have sufficient…no, *ample* wealth. Teach me
the ways of a good steward and a faithful servant. Let
my money follow my heart for You. Use my resources
to bring blessing to others. You richly provide, Lord—
I am investing in Your hope.

# What a Life Produces

*Our people must learn to devote themselves to doing
what is good, in order that they may provide for daily
necessities and not live unproductive lives.*

—TITUS 3:14

I have been devoted to a number of things over the
years. Sadly, a few of them were passing fancies, trendy
needs. And I learned a lot from their demise. Lord, You
are my one true devotion. Help me take the next step
after loving You: following You.

Cultivate in me a character of decency. Let me work
hard and carry out deeds of kindness. May Your seeds
of grace fall on fertile soil in my heart so a harvest of
honor is later reaped. I pray that I would turn Your
provision into continuous seasons of productive goodness. I want to live a life pleasing to You and beneficial
to others. Direct me in Your ways and keep my spirit
burning with devotion.

# Completed by Love

*No one has ever seen God; but if we love one another,*
*God lives in us and his love is made complete in us.*

—1 JOHN 4:12

About that good work You are doing in me, Lord—
I see that its purpose is far bigger than my single path.
As all of Your children commit to love one another, our
lives become holy together. Help me to truly love my
neighbor as myself. When I look at everyone who is a
neighbor in my life—co-workers, drivers in the next lane,
grocery-store clerks—I think of Your hope dwelling in
each of us.

Lord, as I stand before another person, point out
to me their God-qualities. Show me their special gifts.
Guide me to reach out to their heart in understanding.
Remind me that I am looking at the face of God. May
I join with You to complete this good work called love.

**One-Minute Prayers™ for Busy Moms**

Whatever the age of your children, you will enjoy this sanctuary of simple prayers and inspirational verses. Amid the scheduled, the unscheduled, and all the other demands of family, a minute with God will free you to

- find joy in everyday events
- see God's reflection in your children
- create a life that feeds your family spiritually

**The Power of a Praying® Woman**
Stormie Omartian

Stormie has led nearly 2 million women into deeper, more fulfilling prayer lives. In *The Power of a Praying® Woman,* through her knowledge of Scripture and candid examples of her own epiphanies in prayer, she shows you how to

- draw closer to God
- know His plans and purposes for your life
- receive comfort, help, and strength for every day

Trust Him moment by moment with the concerns of your heart and discover the awesome power of prayer will release in *your* life.